NIGHT CONVERSATIONS WITH NONE OTHER

*For Beth, Peter + Kate,
in goodwill,
from Shreela,
Hendrik
Gawain + Kalin*

SHREELA RAY

cover design: Susan M. Kemp

© **1977** Shreela Ray

The American Dust Series #6

Library of Congress Cataloging in Publication Data

Ray, Shreela.
   Night conversations with none other.

   (American dust series ; #6)
   Poems.
   I. Title.
PS3568.A923N5   811'.5'4   76-39788
ISBN 0-913218-32-4
ISBN 0-913218-31-6 pbk.

$2.95/paper ISBN 0-913218-31-6
$6.95/cloth ISBN 0-913218-32-4

DUSTBOOKS
BOX 1056
PARADISE, CA 95969

for Galway Kinnell

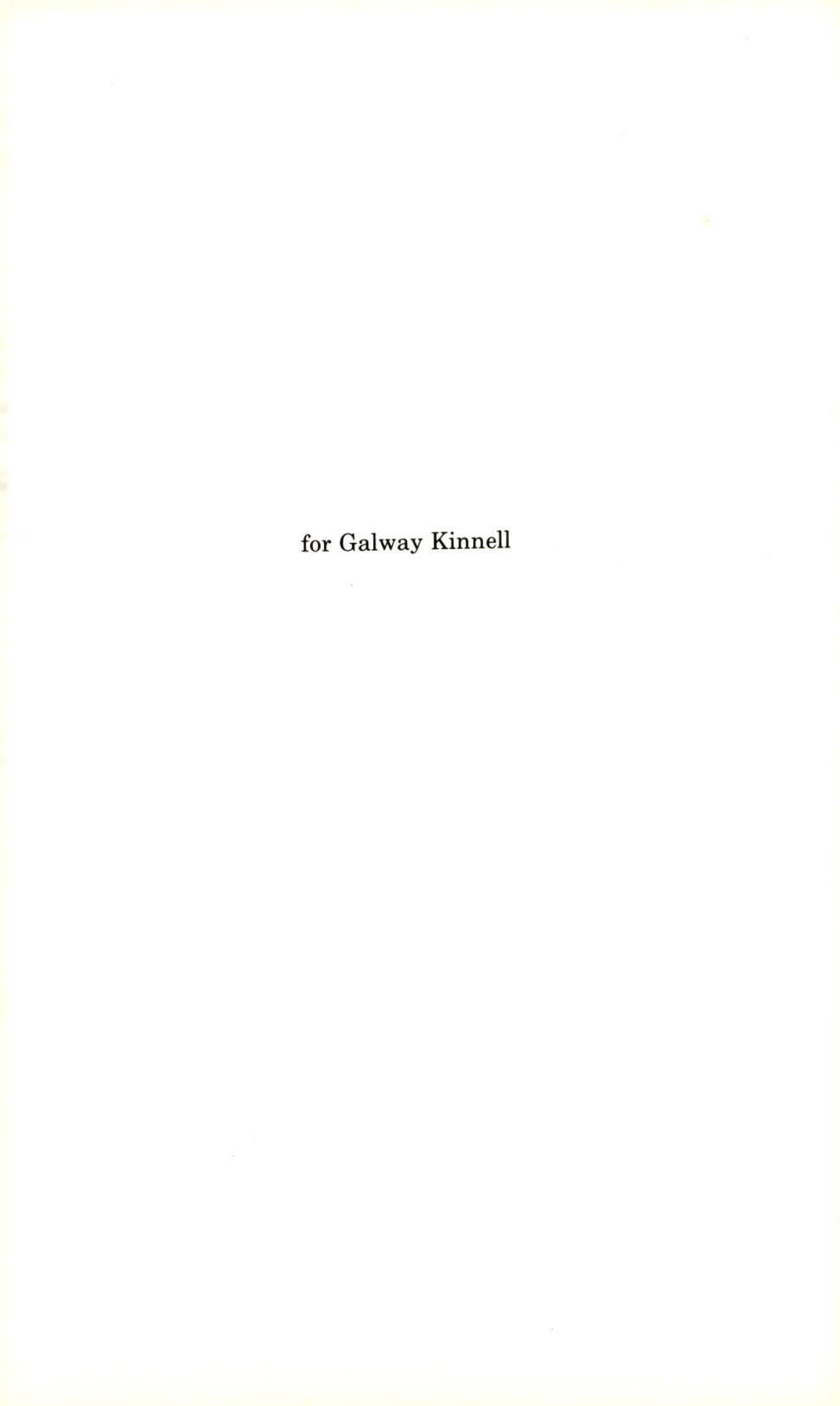

NIGHT CONVERSATIONS WITH NONE OTHER

Acknowledgements:

Some of the poems have appeared in *CHOICE, Out of Sight, The Nation, Southern Poetry Review, Audit-Poetry, Pembroke Magazine, Rapport, Micromegas, The Gray Book* (India), *The Beloit Poetry Journal, Guppie Fancier's Quarterly, CAPstan.*

"For H. Three Poems" first appeared in *The Niagara Magazine,* "Poem", in *The Minnesota Review,* "A Miniature for Hemant Kumar", "Towards a 32nd Birthday", "Poem for Gawain", "Anniversary Poems (5)", in *The Falcon,* "A Manner of Attachment", "Remembering Michaelangelo's David" in *Poetry,* "Letter Home" in a broadside by *The Slow Loris Press,* "The Last Poems", in *Street Magazine.* Many of these poems were written while under grants from the Creative Artists Public Service Program and the Ingram Merrill Foundation.

Special Acknowledgements:

I would like to give special thanks to William Meredith and Sister Jean Carmel who have been patient friends and teachers to me during all my years in America. I would also like to thank Alan Jones for making copies of my manuscript, Mother Joseph Loreto, Peter and Alice McWalters and finally, Jack and Barbara Wolf for proofreading and assembling my manuscript and for other acts of psychological terrorism without which this book would never have been marketed.

Table of Contents

five virgins and the magnolia tree 1

a manner of attachment 2

Night Conversations with None Other 3

Letter Home 4

Poem (for my Father) 5

Jittoku 11

Poem for Sunbathers 12

A Miniature for Hemant Kumar 15

Poem for Gawain 16

Notes from the East 20

For H. Three Poems 24

Winter Poems for Gawain 27

Anniversary Poems 33

If I could win you with a song 38

The Lovers 39

Night in April 40

Ruby Clare by Ruby Clare 41

The Actress on Her Role 44

at a party 46

Two Love Poems Of A Concubine 47

towards a 32nd birthday 48

A Winston Churchill Commemorative 49

Jack Anderson's column, <u>D & C</u> 13/10/74 50

Saul: Four Poems 51

Remembering Michaelangelo's **David** 56

Quasimodo 57

Absence and Others on Main Street 58

To Love 61

An Elegy 63

From a Willow Cabin 65

Maudite 70

Breakthrough 72

The Last Poems 74

Haunting the Dead 76

Poem 78

Allhallows Eve I 79

Allhallows Eve II 81

Letter from a School Friend 83

In Praise of the Beauty of Asian Women 86

The Bondswoman: Three Poems 88

Notes from Underground 91

Monk's Girl in Two Prespectives 93

New Year's Eve 1974 94

Dusky Sally 95

Asia 96

Hour of Darkness, Hour of Light 97

Address Before an Empty Assembly 98

"The windows are open/ and the sleepy violets of the blood/ stir towards the dark outside." These lines from Shreela Ray's beautiful poem "Night in April" describe the process of her poetry. "The windows are open" there in her work, and the sometimes gently, sometimes violently awakened creative intuitions of her interior life ("violets of the blood") move towards the responding "dark" inside each of us.

Ms. Ray is a native of India who has been living in this country for fifteen years, and her work therefore shows the influence of both lands. Her knowledge of Indian places and of Indian gods gives richness to her diction, while her expatriation gives a special turn to that sense of exile which we all feel to a certain extent. Indeed, Paul Tillich described original sin as that very sense. "It is possible that I have come too far," writes Ms. Ray. "The moor, the gypsy and the saint/ are left behind in mysterious union with cripples and thieves./ I sit stiff and upright in the chair/ and drink to them alone./ I bless them, I write for them/ but the song can't find the way back."

There is a brilliant sense of image and of language in these poems. She writes, "The March snow is with us/ between the two stalled maples./ Its rude white silence glitters." Another poem, "Quasimodo," must be quoted entire to show this gift:

> No longer able to believe in God
> I ascend to the angels floating
> in all the rooms of my head.
>
> They are princely and opalescent.
> Their wings fold and unfold in the slow
> motion of an appeal. They thicken
>
> as in its pure arc the spine prepares
> to cut, to multiply, to listen
> for the red heart's chime, endlessly, endlessly.

Difference of skin color is often a visual sign of difference of race; Ms. Ray uses this very movingly in the imagery of her poems. For example, in one of a strong series of pieces for her "Halfbreed child" Gawain, the son of her marriage to a Caucasian American, there is a special poignancy which she catches in her reference to Plato's **Symposium:** "If you should meet Aristophanes first/ ask him, when a man goes in search/ of his sundered female half,/ must she be of the same race?" And in "Two Love Poems of a Concubine," which articulates the pain we all feel at rejection after love, there is an extraordinary twist of the knife in words reflecting the difference of color between the two lovers:

1

Crawling into the black box on the wall
I call myself in the name
of fathers and friends and lovers
and most of all
in the name of one whose face
engraved on a stone turns
away from me and looks
into its heart.

2

Afterwards
when you turn your white back to me
I lie awake in the dark remembering your words.
"I wanted to keep some distance between us."
Had I no rights? Was something
wrong with me? I touch
my Indian body lightly . . . .

Yet every man or woman, trapped inside his own skin, inside his own religion or neurosis, is seemingly of a different "race" from every other — indeed, sometimes we can be so split from our own selves that it is as if each of us were of a different race or color, even from oneself. Poetry, like love, can bridge these great suffering gaps in our experience — that is one of its functions, and Shreela Ray's poems perform this function extremely well.

Ms. Ray has a number of honors to her credit: scholarships and grants from the **Atlantic Monthly,** the Ingram-Merrill Foundation and the New York State Council on the Arts. Ms. Ray has published widely, and she has received recognition from the Discovery Program of the YM-YWHA Poetry Center in New York City. **Night Conversations With None Other** should bring her the greater audience and the greater celebration her poems so surely deserve.

John Logan
Honolulu

five virgins and the magnolia tree

When we were seventeen or sixteen
and sat in the tennis courts
under the Magnolia Campbellii
-- one of the largest flowering trees in the world --
we had lost our senses and we talked our heads off.

Two were to be doctors!
Two students of literature!
One was about to die
and so could not make plans
to heal the world.

Except for her
I forgot the whole lot of you
and of what we spoke
in those hours between
Study Hall and Benediction.

And the good nuns --
if they only knew what
I remember
in the nights of this runaway exile -

the sweet, rich scent,
the cream and white of the magnolia blossom
eight inches across
and blooming strong
way above my head --

they would cut that tree down.

a manner of attachment

Come into the sunlight before me
a little longer . . . .
or are you afraid
of the parallax
light would perform?

Come into the sunlight anyway
for what have we touched
we could lose . . . .
an odd piece of love without hands
from the wrong side of the world.

Night Conversation with None Other

Too many wise damn fools tell me
you will come in time
frosty visitor.
Time is long and so is death
and there is left
the meantime to pass nobly.

The earth in me cries:
sleep-walking child
dropping his dreams
one by one.
Be gentle
gentlemen when
I shall have become too beautiful
ascending
seabird of the deepest
undivulged coffers of the sea
ascending
up
high
to nowhere
that is here
there, nor you.

- for Louis Tsen

letter home

As the outward signs of winter leave us
the purple crocus springs up
in the neighbours yard and on the pavement
pieces of broken beds and picture
frames lie in a heap.

Your life is marked
with no lesser executions:
heat, rain, ice,
births and broken wrists,
deaths imagined and not imagined.

From time to time
let me hear from you.
"In June I shall sit for the examinations
There is talk of marriage in December."

But if word of me arrives during
the rains and the rivers turn gray,
I send my bitter angel to guide
you. Let your letter say,
"We have lost the records of your birth
and departure. Nobody
misses you in Bhubaneswar."

Poem (for my Father)

With my sari hiked above my knees
I trip over a stone near
the street. The blood trickles
from one knee in a thin stream.
Outside the gate the men carrying
their burden of death
stop and rest.

She is Durga the terrible one,
Kali, the Black Mother,
her title —
the ferry across the ocean of existence.
Her long tongue is red with human blood.
She wears a girdle of human arms
and a necklace of human heads.
On either side of her, her
handmaidens grin as they tear
the limbs of children, and eat.

I go closer.
I have seen her beautiful
by another name;
dainty and small beside her husband.
Those about to die wear
a look of indifference almost
as they fold their hands in that gesture
of farewell, or greeting or supplication.

Goddess, Mother, Durga,
before the rivers deliver you to the ocean
already red with the blood of Asia,
I offer you one bleeding knee,
like straws my last two hands

to add to your ten. My wrists
have opened and closed four times
so I could see what the springs
of my body generate. In my
time I have also known galleries
of angels and demons.
Lady of harmonies, couple
my north and south.

2

The air is full with the noise
of crows and caterpillars dropping
from the moringa trees,
and the evening sky is red with dust,
dust of the city
dust of the river
dust of paper mills
dust of processions and
pollen dust and dust
of Tulsipur.

From a neighbouring roof
a gramophone blasts out
the latest film hits
and from somewhere below me
a gentler voice sings,
perhaps by design —

What a stranger you are in your own land.
What a disgrace to forget you own language.

I have deserved no less.
Because of the malice
my right foot bears my left
I stay and listen to the end of the song.

Why do you drift through unknown streets?
Whose house will you make your home in?

The weight of the night crushes
your chest. Radius and ulna separate.
The moon passes through your eyes.
Father I am shouting
can you hear me?
The dead do not know english.
They are the true asians who lose
nothing but their lives and die
acre by acre.

You saw my fear go after itself
to learn the cause of all estrangements:
the first hunger and death.
What golden fawn, what book what
song could send me out like this,
cocky and dumb and so afraid?

You should have married me off at sixteen;
or if I was too ugly then
at twenty in the hope that time
would improve me: or if not then
at twenty-eight to an old marwari who needed heirs.
I had hoped to read to you
but my words are impaled in the silence
and only the centipedes moving
among the brown rotting flowers
hear the scream and are heedless.

In the first flowering of grief,
I believed in rebirth.
The second time the loam dries
and the scales fall from my eyes
I swear
to serve the sick and hungry,
to toil the land,
to pray to Jesus
and if I marry
to marry of my own people

and never go to America
or if I do, to throw myself
like a burning page
into her rivers of oil.
Certainly I will forget
all this foolishness of poetry.

I remain where I am.
In the dark sleep of August
your bones take root and seek
my house and I in my half
sleep, with one hear to the ground
hear the endless, soft hum.

3

Hearing of my arrival the squatters
wait burdened with melons and potatoes
at the edge of the forest.
I climb out of the jeep and go to them.
They see I am wearing trousers
and my hair is in a scarf.
They encircle me and salute me as your son.
The women wail and fall upon my neck
with their children, wide-eyed and shy
clinging to their legs.
Shamed already by their gifts
I do not tell them
I am only a girl.

Outside the circle an old man
with a stick in his hands
murmurs to himself,

*The great man's son is always great
even when he is small
and the poor man's son is always small
even when he is great.*

I see the circle tightens.
Beyond it is the jungle without roads
and soon it will be dark.
In the whites of a child's eyes
there are strong thin red ropes.

4

In the rice field a farmer points
to the elephant tracks and turd
scorched by the sun. A soft
warm wind moves through the fields.
There is a faint hum, a rustle
and my hair caresses my face.
I stand under the lookout from where
at night, the labourers armed with fireworks
watch for elephants.
But still they come
and crush the ripe grain
and raise their trunks to the sky
and glean the stars and feed
with the one hand which also
drinks and breathes and seeks.

A bullet would do the job I think,
or is it true
as it is believed in the Cameroons,
that a man shares his soul
with wild animals, a cow
elephant, his bush soul.
If it is true
they do not forget
they would trespass again:
move their great shadows through
the ready grain and repeat the motions
of elephants in flesh.
The ghosts of fathers and grandfathers watch.

5

I do not know how I will die.
Maybe with a gift of flowers,
my head in a noose of jonquils.
Maybe as I step out of a car.
Maybe (it is often too possible)
by my own hand, shot, stabbed
for love or something hazardously
like it. Maybe even murdered.

My bush soul returns
carrying the cone and spearhead in my groin:
feeding in the cities and granaries
of this continent and shadowing
my hunter.

Who would want to hurt me?
This vast, black and kindly frame
that has stood on its hindlegs,
balanced balloons on its snout
and amused your children.
I have carried you and your burdens
and seen my body divided.
Here is a table from a foreleg,
a head gazes impassively from a wall,
the roses of my tusk grace a wrist, an ear.
But I do not come for revenge;
only to see the face of the hunter
and to reassemble myself.
If there is one here who knows me
give me the spear a second time
a third until I am
my own faintest memory.

Jittoku

... a Buddhist mystic, laughing at the moon.

attr. to Geiami, 1432-1485,
Japanese Ashikaga Idealistic.
Museum of Fine Arts, Boston

The mystic Jittoku takes a rest
from his chores. He lays his broom
by his thonged feet and mound of dust
to stand under the casuarina tree
and gaze at the moon.

And the moon is pale,
barely visible in the pale sky
five hundred years old,
and so is Jittoku by now,
still on his break
with his hands behind his back
and hidden in long flowing silk sleeves
they wore in those days.

The wind blows the scraggy branches
above his head and his thatch of black hair.
The wind swirls the dust and leaves
round and round as he
leans forward respectfully
and laughs at the moon.

I take my break
and look hard at my sky
and specially hard at the moon
full and bright as mother-of-pearl.

No, no, Jittoku, I say
this must be a different one.

Poem for Sunbathers

> "O Sun, make me dark."
> A young woman's prayer
> by a swimming pool.

Then there's the one about this village
whose entire population was afflicted
with a terrible dark disease.
It made them itch, it gave them sores
for years —
they prayed to God
to save them from the itch, the sores,
the exterminating forays of health officials
from the Metropolis.

And one young girl prayed specially,
"O God, how can the health officer's son
notice me
when I look like this?"

But on her twenty-second year she gave up
prayer, pilgrimage, puja.
She lit a fire by a mirror
to look at herself in —
on a piece of paper began to record
(with illuminations)
daily,
the progress of her sores,
their exact size, shape and discolourations,
the varying intensity of the burning,
at sunrise, midday and after dinner.

She took singing lessons.

Then one day
tired of the tears
and the whining of the villagers
God came down
from the sky
with a sack
and went from house to house,
collecting the afflictions, sores, itches.

At last He came to the house of the woman
(by now nearly blind, old and one big sore)
and found her by her fire,
singing to her image in the mirror,
which by now was also old
and had lost much of its silver.

And God told her who He was
and what He was doing there.

And she remembered herself at eighteen,
leaving her father's house
with one pair of sandals
and an ancient, black winter coat
bought on Bond Street by her aunt.
She remembered the corpses
of an uncle, a best friend turning to sand.

And she remembered herself at twenty-two
following the grey eyes
of the health officer's son
looking past her
at the imported clock tower.

And she ordered God
to get the hell out of her house,
which He did.
The dim view
of God's backside
pleased her
more than even the health officer's
son would have,

which only goes to show
there's more to life than a case
of unrequited love.

Anyway,
because of her
the village was re-infected.

A Miniature for Hemant Kumar

The March snow is with us
between the two stalled maples.
Its rude white silence glitters.

I will not come to terms.

I back up.
The glass behind me breaks:
ropes of red onions scatter on the floor,
but I never take my eyes off
and retreat.

Your pure voice, Hemant Kumar,
that once could drug my peevish self
and make me move
once in the sunlight
once in the evening
like a dancer —
keens for an alien.

Hai Babu,
I should care
if the sun warms the fields and Radha's feet,
or that spring comes again to Kashi and Brindaban.

Poem for Gawain

1

Half-breed
child
you are the colour of the earth,
limbs of trees and deep rivers.
Only in them can you find sanctuary.

You remind me of my country,
its divisions, its inalterable destiny;
the white sands of Puri turning red,
the Deccan a tableland for scavengers.

I would like to save you,
to search for a second home.
There is none
because we are the poor
and the elders of the earth.
So use my body as a shield
and behind its metal sing
of the dark, so when death comes
you will think it is the sea.

And this casket, this body,
lie on it,
warm, familiar,
as though you were in your own room,
in your own bed.

2

If you should find yourself
one day
in love with a Chinese girl
in a cafe in Paris,
do not tell her
to stay with her own people,
even tenderly.

Follow her home,
stand under her window in the rain
but on no account give her
five dollars and send her off
in a taxi.
She may have more sense
and decide to go on living anyway.

And if you should meet Aristophanes first,
ask him,
when a man goes in search
of his sundered female half,
must she be of the same race?

3

I stand in the heartland.
From the south the ocean breaks in.
The desert blows towards the centre.

I do not know what to call it;
suicide, or murder or the natural
course of things,
when the wretched fall upon the wretched
for guns or for bread.

I will write this story for you
on a tortoise shell comb,
where the song becomes

something old and slow and hidden
in the carapace of your tiny
mortality.

4

What will you do?
You are the gold around my neck.
Star —

Learn American-English
live long
and be strong
and gun your mother down.

5

My father was buried alive
in the paddy fields
by his International Harvester tractor.
When they dug him out
his face was calm and he seemed
to be smiling.
How could I be sure
that mud hadn't transformed his mouth
and that the juice and grass of his land
hadn't masked his face?

For thirteen years I have carried
dead fathers, grandfathers, uncles
and the virgin halves of myself
in search of friendly ground.

Even the graveyards have no entry
for Marxist poets . . . .

So I buried them all
in my head.

6

Mist in the morning
and mist over the hands below me
loading and reloading
mysterious shipments from the east.
Not the ancient commodities —
cloves and silk, but the heavy stuff
for the dinners and security
of the United States of America.

I start thinking about God.
At a time like this.
Above all things
in a place like this:
I think Bellona Christ is the greatest of gods.
He has even joined the Israelites.
All we ask of Buddha
is that he lie on his side
so we can carve lotus blossoms
on the soles of his feet.

I will speak of this always,
sometimes as we watch for the dawn
and the paper, and I see the red and blue
flag with its one white star
I cut with my own hands,
wrap itself around our makeshift staff.

I cannot tell you enough
that I am frightened.
My life is like the wastelands
Amerika leaves behind her.
And a people cannot be saved from this
by nails or sabbaths or chemistry
when every new infant is cradled
in the jawbone of an ass
bleached in that desert.

Notes from the East

1

My small time despair settles
like the anopheles mosquito
on this paper
and infects it.

2

I have no stones in my
pockets to keep me down.
A piece of the Russian's mouth
falls at my knees —
these two clubs
that have not bent
for prayer or pardon in a long time.

And because at last you said you would come
on the 21st of March, 1974,
my son and I waited
all afternoon, the night,
the next morning.
Even the phone didn't ring.

He drew a picture for you.
You have yellow hair and yellow eyes.
The letter 'G' marks your chest
in red and blue.
Above your head he leaves a vast
untouched sky of white paper.

He fell asleep.
When he awoke he asked,
"Are they here yet? Did they come
and go while I slept?"

His hair smells of coconuts,
his skin of turmeric and mustard oil.
I wonder how long it will take
to breed out his accidents.

For my crime of believing in good manners,
for my sins against my husband and Bob Casto,
for my failed attempts at biothanatos,
for thinking my yoni as good as any
in these fifty states,

Amerika, you shall not touch my son.

This little boy
conceived on an island in Maine
came out bloodless —
a hybrid waterlily
from the eye of hell.
He cried in many tongues
when his darknes and mine
thrust him out
into this guise of light,
this USA.

But he has hurt no one.
Gawain the kind,
Gawain the courteous and gentle knight.

There was strength in these veins.
It has mixed with water —
a little more each day.
Lord, if mercy dries me up,
I will turn to law.

Can there be comfort for a heavy smoker? —

The gods, the gods are everywhere.
They move in packs
and I smoke them out
in the bathroom where I lock myself.

Take me to your leader.

Allah?
Ram?
Yahve?

What **is** your name?
Where do you live?
What is your number?

Why did the black girl sleep in the pines?
Show me the way to go home.
Forget everything and do that
one.

That is impossible for reasons
you have already explained to your physician.

Ah.
My physician. (A long pause.)

Dear Saint
Mother Theresa,
please do not anticipate my services.
I have sprouted breasts.

Hump-backed creature/soul,
I drink your milk,
fight fire with urine
and use it as tonic; salve
the wounds which open
everytime the desert takes
the shape of a friend
fleeing the sandstorm.
Ultimately
I tear the throat's rancid sac
and drain it.

Whatever happened to Zenobia,
self-styled Queen of the East?

The sand in your eye
was once a part of her.
Examine it closely.

If it is a part of her brain,
you will go mad.
If it is a part of her once-copious womb,
destroy it immediately.
If it is a scrap of her heart,
there is no knowing what may happen.
In any case,
give it to the boy
and he will plant it in a place of honour
in the potter's field.

For H. Three Poems

1

Leaning

against your sleep —
white body
white
daemon —
I forgive you

In this castle — your arms
I who am an arsenal
against myself —
in this moment
in this sleep
in this ceasefire

a garden is possible even
on Akbar Road
and I know the name of the ship
that will take us there.

2

In the times we are together
I have no self
or memory
of you,
colour and texture,
time or music,
not even poetry.

Let me look at you
in the half-light
and turn slowly, slowly
to the left
and wait
and turn a little more
and wait again.

When I look at you
I feel rich and lazy:
giver of rice and love.

3

You know
I have loved before this
many times,
and once
specially

and still you keep me,
keep me
in rice and loving.
And there is nowhere I can go
without your mark,
these rivers,
roots and trees
on my groin.

Winter Poems for Gawain

the first one

We stand together at the window
in the room where I write these poems,
in the room where you play ball
with my crumpled castaways.

And we watch the trees sway
like two files of monks
passing each other on the road.
The west wind howls against the windows.
If we let it in, it would make sails
of our bedding and leave us both behind.

I carry your small body
to your bed and lie with you
in the dark. This is our time.
We are the only two other
dark things in the room
and what I tell you now
is not in your books of alphabets
or kind green monsters.

You might return to earth
sooner than you think.
Stay on the right side of trees —
they can lift you up in a flood,
and let a snowflake spend
its short life on your hand
or bury itself in your eyes.
It cannot hurt you
and you may learn something.

You are the same but not the same.
You will not have time to say,
I do not know or wish to know,
or
What can I do.

Angel, the sound of rustling moths
is unlike the sound of trucks and railroad cars,
and the smoke of apple wood unlike the smoke
of wool and wet leaves and the smell
of buring rubber unlike burning oil
and burning flesh.
Anything can happen again
if you are not careful.

the second one

Every snowflake
is an arrangement of knives.
I have cut my heart out.
Suet for the birdhouse.

So my son,
when I say get lost
it means I will follow you
soon.

Haven't you guessed by now
if I hang around
it is only because
you haven't
got lost.

the third one

Yes.
It is almost winter
and it will snow any day.
I cannot think of the summer
nor do I dream
of what you dream of
against me,

against the pencil rack
of my breasts.

Against me

I trace your eyebrows
like two thin moons,
fur scythes.

Who will be the first
like the thief in the night?

This then is my wish,
this my dream for the winter —
let it be you
so I can say,
"By the moon in its first quarter
was I cut down."

the fourth one

Here are more lies
so I can live a little longer.

You must be the success
I never thought of at fifteen.
There is no hint of failure
in your kiss, of second best,
the understudy. You do not
tell your gratitude to me
and speak of love for other women.

In your each eyelash is a line of kings.

Here is a speaker of the House,
here is a chief minister, a chief justice.
This one built a temple to Lingaraj.
This one went broke for a no-good daughter,

You must believe this, little arab,
for the guns and contempt are pointed east.

the fifth one

Hagar

Darkness,

In this land, failure
is always around the corner.

A girl —
the colour of walnuts, —
eyes like almonds —

reads her list
of services rendered
as if it were a history book.

Praise what you must praise,
and pity what you must —
Hagar —
if you will
imperil your fortunes.

You have moments to remember;
the hope of turning the page for a girl.

She cannot be frightened
by her own kind when he comes nearer
like a priest amid groves and temples.

Feast on almonds.
In your absence be together.

Anniversary poems

1

Whatever that place is
in which you found me,
I do not want to know.
If there was wilderness
there is garden,
if there was sand only,
there is a wheat field,
if there was sadness
there is now dancing.

But look what I have made of this place.

I know I talk as if
my heart is in my shoes sometimes
but see how they plant themselves
in this house, this kitchen,
by this bed.

I grow, I grow
still
a nail of clove
you husband.

2

Perhaps it is true,
as the man said,
I did not choose
but was whipped into this marriage

Now there are two of you
and I still can't tell
need from love.
This pale green
or colourless,
parasitic thing
eats and drinks
at every threat
the flour and blood of your hands.

You know its roots,
you know its claws,
the poem written
out of a sexless, dead-end love
for another man.

3

Take me away from here.
But wherever we go
I want to be certain
that you are with me.

Signs are not enough,
or word either, or hands
or fear, or fear of children
or children
or books

or drink.

Because then
I sniff the child and eat books
and plant hands and serve
music.

In any case it doesn't work.

4

I love you
by all that is light and honeycomb
and sons.
But what is hidden,
and without science or water
is strong also.

And you are a stranger
in the vicinity of the half moon
and the evening rain
and you are then
as nothing —
I don't know you.
I don't care.

5

I shall summon the press, lawyers, judges,
and tell them everything.
But you must not be present.
Your silence will stir them
like the voice of my country,
and the fall of mango blossoms
at nightfall.

I love you
but you must
go
and learn when
after sex there is no sadness,

because now when I turn towards you,
there is a wraith at my shoulder
and her face is like the back
of my hand, so dark, so knotted, so lined.

If I could win you with a song.

When Tansen sang
the sky broke with rains
the candles in the moghul court
guttered and went out.
Even the stones wept.

I am not Tansen
nor is there sky here
worth speaking of
and when the rocks move I hear
the Tic Tic Tic tic tic
of their faultless hearts.

THE LOVERS

Like bats in the valley of shadows
presented to the radiant sunflower,
they do not crave the mercy of eyelids.

They put away the knife from limbs and faces,
mild as children put away other arms.
For the time being their hands are cymbals

as they witness the miracle of the plover
the span of whose ambitions finds room
even in error.

The flower is manifold to them and the music
their own; greater than you or I until
like children caught in the act
of being pleased with their bodies,
they join us in habitual punishment.

Night In April

The voice of the April wind addresses
the unmarriageable awake
in the real sleep of the body.
The windows are open
and the sleepy violets of the blood
stir towards the dark outside;
that final nakedness
in the silhouettes of doorways
and branches ascending and descending.
To stay would mean for always
I would remain to weigh and measure.

Let your breath enflame a second
marriage for that end. As for me
there is some other livelihood
when the essences of things call me 'sister'!

Before I draw back my wings and fall
into the keel of birdlike flowers
by god I will make a garden of this place.

Ruby Clare by Ruby Clare

In the theatre is standing room only.
Put on your shoes girl and your coat.
It is time to go Miss
Ruby Clare
like the red stone,
the rock, and when I say
rock; I mean rock and water
and air, crystal, chocolat
Miss Ruby Clare.

The sun breaks like a bad egg.
Its angel gives one wish.
Gentleness, I said: is there
anyone who knows who
Mirabai and Tansen were?
Let us play Botticelli together.
I think I am closer to you.
I can speak English:
name at least twenty american presidents.
I am perhaps a little too familiar
with first names — john
jean martha bill. My name is Ruby Clare
aunt jemima go comb your hair.

The wind sings throught the casuarinas
at Puri. I guard our shores and watch,
afraid of the great ships coming
against us. My father is a farmer and
every evening he returns from the fields
with a piece of bone caught
by the plough. One day the children
will assemble the pieces and see
What they have:
a monkey, a rabbit, a bear.

It is night.
To it I sign my name.
The savage hump of the darkness
rubs against my breasts.
My ear is his theatre and
willing audience when he speaks
Tell them from me, my friend
the moon has an eye for pitch bones.
Throw dice with your skull, it
always falls face up.
The mud in the socket loosens
and in the jaws.
You can see
the planets slipping.
You have a tongue and can curse.
Send me no more poets.

At the window the curtains flutter,
diaphanous, beige.
They wrap themselves around
an empty wine bottle, the Tibetan
god of blessings wearing
a coronet of skulls.
Assassins and thieves hide behind
a song breaking its heart
for a calcutta orphan. And for
this awards arrive by mail?

George, Mary Gray
Cameron Este's falling down,
3-2-1 all gone.
I say man, all
gone.

I unbutton my blouse as
I sing.
"With her head tucked underneath her arm."
I keep my balance all right.
In the graveyard, the madhouse, no
one worries about being delicate.
In bed sometimes I play
at dying with a sign until
the beauty of geometric designs in the room
brings me back.

I am the daughter of kshatriya.
Soldiers bury me.
The dew takes to the air,
that sweet unnatural country,
and Asia and Africa are my retinue.
But my father why did you let
me go with the only patrimony
I stole from my brother?

The theatre is emptying.
Aging women and widows listen
to an actress talk of love —
a man's genitals. What could
they be thinking of?

It is empty.
All the faces are gone.
Gentleness, I asked
but the lord is a joker.
I have kept my place:
a red stream, pastry.
It is empty so that once even
I may be beautiful.

The Actress on Her Role

As the curtain goes up I have time
to re-arrange myself.
Lady, you had less bosom than sense
but such sense!
Pompey, Ceasar, Antony!

Homely and painted I die for Antony.
Antony? What Antony?
I believe you lied.

I abide by necessity, not
the antic heart.
I hitch up my breasts and go forth.

The Valley is attentive to my physique
for your words are strange;
this pose unfit
for impermanence or death although
nobody quite believes it anymore
and nor do I

at least not since
I was 18 and silly with desire.
I have learned to joke at your expense.
A world must be kept in order;
the children must be scrubbed and fed,
the bills paid, the frantic bitch locked in.

My husband . . .
his life . . .
a thing apart . . .

and yet —
in the sleep of my old age I listen for
a market humming with astonishment and praise,
envious unmarried girls.

Come.
Your time is up.
The asp must attack
and you triumph in death.
(Over the sink I keep a phial
should the going get too rough.)

Easy poor queen
Remember what it is you die for . . .
I cannot.

I touch your hand.
Royal Egypt, farewell.

                                            for Isabella

at a party

From room to room I go
in search of you. There are vine
leaves in my hair. Habitually all things
in your way must fall.

What can I tell you now if you come —
that I will be afraid today and the green
robe fall loose from my fingers no matter
how often, I have rehearsed and rehearsed the scene.

Two Love Poems Of A Concubine

1

Crawling into the black box on the wall
I call myself in the name
of fathers and friends and lovers
and most of all
in the name of one whose face
engraved on a stone turns
away from me and looks
into its heart.

2

Afterwards
when you turn your white back to me
I lie awake in the dark
remembering your words.

I wanted to keep some distance between us.

Had I no rights. Was something
wrong with me? I touch
my indian body lightly.
My answer comes
in the shape of a woman without breasts
who holds two smooth stones in her hands.

*I am deformed and black
and greater than your sadness.*

My anger is bound to my pride
with silk threads. I look
to the footboards and headboards
for saints to lift me up
to high safe places
for I know I know
if I lie in all the beds
of this world
I sleep with one man
who has his back to me.

towards a 32nd birthday

On Route 33 East
in the late afternoon,
after the rain, the fields
are half-lit by a strange sunlight
breaking through gray clouds.

Hobbema's 'The Avenue Middleharniss'.

I grow afraid of my dreams —

you fleshed out in the thicket, suddenly,
returning to redress
eight years of my grievances;
my self-made
phalanx of bodyguards;
Tobias' angel turns away,
the fish stink,
the smooth gray stones
cold and hard
have lain under the peepul tree.
Theirs is a journey I may never make.

So I cry when they speak out,
in that natural secret voice
without judgement or accent
by all my names.

Foreigner

woman
mother
wife

jongleur.

The sun's waning shaft hangs above us all
like the sword of the other
archangel.
If it falls it would cut the road in half.

A Winston Churchill Commemorative

I commemorate that pink hoof
held up in a 'V'.

Winston Churchill,
Sir,
a man despised by half the world
and honored with citizenship
by this country.—

Eat your heart out Ezra Pound.

Jack Anderson's column <u>D & C</u> *

Inside the huge public square of my heart
a crowd gathers.
The people are shouting and carrying signs:—
Long live the poppy fields!
A 100-watt light bulb in every hut!
Get out of my house!

I can tell by their complexion
they will all be eliminated.
I despair and fall asleep.
Still,
last night a group of them
climbed aboard a freighter
and dumped entire crates of Coca-Cola
into the harbour.

* Democrat & Chronicle

Saul: Four Poems

1

*And Saul said unto him, Why
have ye conspired against me, thou
and the son of Jesse . . . ?*
1 Samuel, 22, v. 13.

The room begins to take the shape of a vault.
A storm lashes the trees,
I try to keep my head as cool
as a vegetable garden in the summer heat
when the forked spirit longs to put
herself together and be still.

Last night I sat biting my nails
and cried like a girl in her time of month.
Tonight I broke the clock in trying to set it right.

The darkness sits on the chair and purrs and yawns.
In the cat's infernal retina
someone is drowsing and I am no lioness to lay
my imperious length against the cub.

There is nothing of the cat about me:
the sleek body, the green eyes,
the cat habit of licking itself clean.
I only let him in as an old man forgetfully allows
angels or patience room in his house.

Thou knowest these things Lord
but I will speak.
If the gadfly does not know the whereabouts of the abyss,
the hand I beware, hold.

2

Epithalamion

The slightest brush of wings
sets the spirit humming,
swarming with stars.
When Orion unbuckles his belt
and rains the stars upon my head
there is no business wanting the dead.

The cyclamen of the year is under snow;
filament and another — ash.
Snow is ash,
woman and child,
ash is ash . . . .
things   I have touched.

How greedily they devour the blackness
and are devoured.
They never cry or grow absurd.
Your gold bangle brands the nape of my neck.

I am disturbed . . . .
Is that blackness light?
have you forgotten you were snow-haired at birth?
I turn to salt and ash.

Armies of flies settle
upon the cut melon of our summer
to taste the red and sweet of our trouble
with satisfaction.

I have loved — it is true,
but it was nothing.
That you are gone is true
but it does not matter.

Besides, you would not like the taste of my mouth.
It tastes too much of nettles and indignation.

This is the hardest of all,
that we cannot choose to sacrifice
where the Law has decided.

3

My father when
the Moor stirs the constellations
of a foreign particular sky,
new rivers with his foot,
the eyes of the unkind father
are always upon him.

My father,
how many men in search of their father's asses are made king?

Oh go to sleep and dream no more of daughters.

4

Some part of the sun will surely get us,
or perhaps, it will be the moon.
It does not matter which, so long
as the earth gets no perspective.

It buzzes and spins —
the little earth.

I break like a ship,
a ship of many voyages
and once much loved.

But on the glass bird in the hold
the bright sun breaks and breaks.

Remembering Michaelangelo's <u>David</u>

By these his hands the vineyards ripen
and the beasts rise again in meadows,
tó move off, desiring death again
in another time.

The women still observe him with impassive faces
and ungirdle themselves for the boy.
Old women in the delight of terror.
His eyes . . . .

And dead young girls chafe against the cold,
wake to match the marble and breed
a race of beauty not for death.

How men regard him secretly in their
philistine awe, as he stands above
in anxious and terrible expectancy . . . is it . . .
of kingdoms and years of men.

He arrives always at the exact marble word
and the entire stone slays
the preposterous giant. When it roars
why should he care, this boy
who holds the covenant.

Quasimodo

No longer able to believe in God
I ascend to the angels floating
in all the rooms of my head.

They are princely and opalescent.
Their wings fold and unfold in the slow
motion of an appeal. They thicken

as in its pure arc the spine prepares
to cut, to multiply, to listen
for the red heart's chime, endlessly, endlessly.

Absence and Others on Main Street

These . . . .

from a well-stocked earth;
flies, footprints, crow's feet
the greater half of man and how many
creatures dead in the arms of time.

The only sun and I at noon
go mad, so tomorrow when the sun rises
this devious and cat blood
will be modified by its ninth death.

There are those who will always be after
pale centres of pistil, white stamen, yes,
in the ethical climate of these hemispheres.

But how far the wind carries
the dust of wild weeds:
capsules of poppy burst
and send here, there.

And what is the lord's plan
in the hip of the dark solitary rose?

And you know the way back.
Tarmac and planes overhead.
Flowers.

One belongs to convolvulus and one
compositae and one I
should know best, the inadequate
flowers.

The Scholiast
wrote of you Sappho as having been
very ugly, small and dark
but like the nightingale with deformed wings
enfolding a tiny body.

Sappho, a song before you drown
for the ferryman, a song
even for the girl who walks
in the scent of violets.

As for me —
there is always a boy
in the hyacinth
and because one summer in Vermont
I stood among bulrushes
in the water
and suddenly the sun
pared me to the skin.

I felt the green world
like a HE
trip me with one blade

I gathered twelve rushes,
as if the twelve tribes of man
were in my arms,
singing in me.

Why is it wrong to ache for the sea?
Supposing the sun would say

"I am not bright enough,"
and sink fast?
You sleep in the eye of another summer,
whom time foraged and saved and proved

a friend. I speak and raise
the black rib of the phone
turning seashell in my hand,
and the shell in the ear awakes
and listens and moves at the sound
of the gentlest sea, far off.

I dread afterwards —
you would look on me
twisted and rotten
on a New England shore

and say,
"Is this your sea?
The evergreen?
The way arms should hold?
Answer me.
Even the waters turn you back."

In sleep the indwelling sunflower is brightest.
The coquina is washed by the sea,

until he comes on gravel, his bruised
leg ascending the stair, his frayed
sleeve wiping his forehead.

Nothing is the same as before.

To love

The smoke goes out the window taking
its proper time.

Mine is no mineral heart like yours,
sinister, unwilling, oddly
brave. This is not what I
was saved for, to be lice in your hair
so pluck me out and leave
for another country,
the blonde, the beautiful.

I would retire if I only had
a summer of his care.

2

What is this made of?
Marble? Granite? Diamond?

Analyse.
Analyse everything:
volcanic ash and under the
microscope the culture changes during
the four hours you
do not watch most of all.

I have seen young boys dedicated
to collecting butterflies.
I saw monarchs and swallowtails,
New Guinea Goldens etherised
and pinned to cardboard.

3

Your great heart will crack,
the marrow weaken. With no little
love I tell you this. What little
I have. I thought a poet would care
for even such things.

The sublime —
have you seen it anywhere?
Your night words fall over me.
I gather them and clothe you;
this is not so, not so.

But when I lisp and stutter
you suspect the lie and even as this
body I hold.

Good bye and so allons.
Hang on to the key.
The conclusion bars applause,
for what man reveres another
before he invades him?

Think nothing but blackness:
not so deficient as the distance
from here to there. It outcultures
my life: its full moons,
successions and the pathological
use of words.

Had I the moon in my lap
I would outrun you all.

An Elegy

At last they uncoil, hold
bark, gum, a naked field
dandelion. The river does not stop
the fit. To falter,

to think is not
the moment. Winds hurl down
an ounce of god, a loose rock,
the mountain weed, flower
of shattered stem.

They come after me, the birds, and spread
like elegies in a wood too dense
for undertaking, even alone.

Collector bees grow lazy.
Already the flies buzz. The earth cracks
where the worms toil

in one who dreamed of requital,
the sea or where rich sap
whelms stronger pines,
and the seed in the brain is permitted to bloom

without the jingle of metal rain, without
this green deep intrusion doomed
to earth's centre.

Louder and louder the greed
of water falling sucks at the nerve
holding me back like
the pickerel caught in weeds.

There is no escape from your unbearable
american benevolence. Let
Asia take her bastard child without complaint.

The waters of seven continents rush
towards me and over me.

2

The camps are silenced at night.
The terrorising Midianites rest.
I go from light to light and come
to one desolate tent without incense

or flowers or hysterical women
and an old father cut down before his time,
and you in another country
thrashing the invincible net

that must imprison you.
I will always be there
bending backwards to see
my mortality reversed,

spitting upon itself . . . .
what you would not touch.

Hands rise against the heavy moon
sinking fast to throat, breast,
thigh now foot tethered to the pole
south of earth and I hear
the wild hungry birds flutter,
and the earth try pulling away.

From a Willow Cabin

It is early morning
and still no dawn. I try
to pass time thinking
of the brow of the Macedon,
the kiss that was Antony's
and full of death . . . .

and you — where I am.

How disagreeable it is — this road
they have me take
                       guarded
by three storms.

There is witchcraft in the wind,
the verging meadows overgrown
with aconite and nightshade.
There is insurrection in the rain.
Not a daisy has promised to be reborn.

Where is delirium or flight?
When they pin me to this black cross
how can I sing or dance?

If I were Nataraj, four arms wouldn't be enough.
My teeth would bite the rain,
these tired lids drink the sunlight I have dreamed.

I ask for fourteen berries of BellaDonna
to fly with the tongue of the meadowlark.

Trees

the un-netted growth
of saga
told tongue to tongue
past our chemistry
unfold once, twice, thrice
in me aimlessly reciting
'light, light' —

coherence.

The genius in the thicket is wild
seeking *the* berry in a bush
crammed with berries.

In the meantime, the Great Star
rises and sets on my back
like the angel of the miraculous pool
who stoops once, to one in a thousand years.

Teach me to be patient as Methuselah
in his eight-hundredth year before Christ.

God, they have barred the earth from me
and anger takes all night to close.

I look out of the window
at those distant possible roses
of twenty-two or twenty-three.

My would-be children cling to my skirts.
What will they do when they learn
I did not nurse them?

Like the moor, I was driven out for spain.

When you left, having nowhere to dive,
I let the fluid poison stain
the minotaur bed. The sword in your eyes
gives you away and I am not quick to move.

I have no guile or occult power
to seize the sun from its centre
and place it on your head or mine.

What do you care anyway for the crown of the sky
when my earth shudders in the light of your stride?

According to the roots of prophecy
the rotting tree was cut down.

The grounds will be perfect when
you walk with her.
The mind will not recall the sick
poisonous sapling of the tropics
only a botanist studies with interest.

The angel of history gave me
this little courage: remembrance
of the shudra Anarkali walled
to death for the love of Salim:
and Daniel delivered from the lion's mouth.

But tell me love, is my voice *so* soft?

At once the vision struck.

I could not wait to ride
the spindrift.
There was no one to stop
or rival me with arguments.

I reject the apocalyptic promise of him
exiled at Patmos till his hair turned gray.

I reject the indifferent metallic blur,
the brick with which this house is made.

I am nothing —
but averse to vegetable cells
and the impossible law which outlaws itself.

It was rain I leaned to hear
or someone shouting in the corridor, "shower!"
meaning the divine gold, the ocean spray?
I delayed at the window to make sure. There wasn't
a drop that even touched me gingerly, like you.

I stare at the trees;
strained to understand the language of osprey,
migrations of domestic birds.

Tell me what is green and earth and rain,
what is mud and sky but do not tell me with words.

I only know a song when it comes
from the lips of old women, demented and crying aloud
to an insensible Polish god, or whining,
"Kiss me nurse, before I sleep."

The night passes me on to disbelief,
and belief in the mercy of killing
them or me. We sing
in different keys.

All night I have watched
the orange flicker jammed
in my breast, smoke out,
be cancelled in the sea

Where dream fish receive
the gift of speech in my tongue
and the last anemone of the world
flowers in my ear.

My fingers turn to water.
A flower opening in its final hour
in the face of you — the Sun —

I am that other presence, a head
of semi-flowers, ray, disc. Burn,
burn for I am strange to the lover's kiss.

Bring me such flowers —
wild poppies.

Maudite

To this unfurnished house I bring myself
and a lamp to write by, a few clothes.
The landlord lent me a roll-away bed
as hard as knuckles and a rocking chair.

On the third floor, under the gables,
the light gives itself to the trees.
The living room is strewn with books,
verses having another day. I look

to the hour I will toll the bells
with my right hand, when the roses
will overwhelm you and the room
be defining Morocco.

In its mystical way
the after-image takes shape.
There is a knock on the door.
There is a voice speaking my name.
There is a whirr where two wheels touch.
There is confusion in the eightfold path to the grail.

What this house needs is a guest.
Many weeks have passed and still there is no word.

Only the book is left.
On a page I read a girl's name.

Without knowing it, the night
that is always with us becomes personal.

Down the long street a begger calls at a name.

The rain falls making
incalculable exceptions. It is the same
rain that is music and sometimes
without heart. It is the rain
that sometimes listens to itself
and cries its small measure.

How coldly the wind rocks the sleepers
in this house; those spectres
on which I breathe,
nil, nil.
And the path still leads to the sea.

Awake I listen for anything
that arrives and rocks and goes,
and think

there is no day when the sun
rises and sets without his knowledge.
and the green and brown earth is light
and ignorant of his weight
(or I am).

There is less than ourselves
between us.

Breakthrough

Summer ends.
I write as I think
of its locus, my life,
home Marvell and the iron beams
in the lavatory, a skipping rope
and am I a christian?

I remember you saying,
"There is a part . . . . I can be gentle."
That is true. I can easily
count the times.

I wait not knowing why.

I know nothing will appear
at the top of the stairs;
no voice call my name
suddenly through the trees.
I answer and do not answer
just the same.

Brood, without tradition;
billboards or better or the unviable
peninsular blood. Nothing
but this jinni and lover, the garnet
in the mind and Agadir.

Much more than this, the longing
in twenty shades of the sea,
longing for the smell of kelp
in which the body burnt
is healed.

That tree that I hugged
and thought
this will bend and touch
me with two branches.

For a moment I was glad
it acted like a tree
and I like myself and that
there was no getting around it.

The Last Poems

The primeval sun flagged and died.

Not a stone stands on stone.
Whatever you call fossil
skeleton of leaf, print of fern
I call rib cage flat against stone.

If you come down to the final stair
you can see the remains of my poltergeist
keeping a daumier eye,
the world and me alive.

In his wake ferocious
co-inhabitors churn in the foreground.

A week before they brought me here
a woman died in this very bed.
Four hours ago you left and I
re-enacted a hundred possibilities.
Suppose the common clock actually had gone
backwards, making its points against you instead.
How would you have acted differently?

Here. There, everywhere
the mouths of full-blown flowers touch my face
and age elegantly for the coming darkness.
Watch.

Your lips are cold.
Only your invisible hand
combs my hair.

For the last time I press to my ears
the shells and listen spellbound
to the earth grinding passage in the sea
and the sea spilling her salt
on her insensate child.

The wind brings its viaticum
to these sorry flowers
and what goes through the slenderest
pipette from you to me.

Mollusk to musk? No.
Wine to vinegar. See
how the water changes
chalk when you breathe.

It is dark.
Spurious flowers and spires are removed
by the genius of night.
An hour slinks by.

Somewhere it is raining or else
this is a threat.
A girl I don't know wished me joy
and limped out of my way.

Haunting the Dead

The pawnbroker has your flute and I
my teeth. The beautiful animal died
like a mouse on its back
with a spike through its heart.

Sleep then.
I listen to the wind blow in your key.
In this city there are none like
you, or home or bread.

These I love are cold.
They never move.
You can't be dead. How is it
under the earth? At the root caps
of grass and the wildflowers acid?

And under the riverbed? Admire
or wonder that I breathe,
or call me *liar*.
But no wind bears your ashes
dark as your hair, your face.

It is cold and hungry here
and your turn to listen.

You left me one autumn day
shedding darkness as a widow sheds
her mourning dress before
a second marriage.

Nobody asks you "come."
But one day among fantastic cypresses I felt
the quivering world become
the apple of *his* eye.

Come.
And you with the terrible eyes say *no*.
And the message of that thunder falls
as quietly but surely as the rain into my lap.

                      for Thomas Angell

Poem

All January this house has shaken to the beams.
The hinges break. The wind will not behave.
Papers crackle and fall, the pictures on the wall
hang crooked. I sit before the pegged god at one
last fling at this fancy learning.

It is no heroic bounce to hell, every
would-be knows; it is just so —
the word does not fit: the heart creams and spreads
and that doesn't do. The turncoat cat of allegory
about the ramparts stalks its winter shape

and fails to dodge the icicles. She casts
an inward eye, comes home with vital organs
ruptured and a neat trick of the bone
for me to whistle through.
I rise and go to the window. I rise.

My fingers are in knots. My self about to break.
Something behind me pulls my hair.
Something behind me laughs and laughs
and pulls me to the chair to crawl to some
beginning when the current breaks.

Allhallows Eve I

Waxed by the mist leaves
hung in that thin space between
earth and sky.
In winter the trees are bare.
The windows rattle and the house
shudders in its frame.
It is an ugly season
but darkness is the time
of diverse tongues.

I must return to my country
for what is Boston to me or New York?
You sleep and do not hear.
Show me to your joys
their recesses, those
woods lit up by aspens.

For it is possible that I have come too far.
The moor the gypsy and the saint
are left behind in mysterious union
with cripples and thieves.
I sit stiff and upright in the chair
and drink to them alone.
I bless them,
I write for them
but the song can't find the way back.

In my house the devils crow.
Their poison is too free although
they speak some sense:
"Let your life be a whip against you, dreamer,"
and so on. They seem to know
more than our idols do,

the origin of song is deep
in the science of things:
the fishbone lodged in the throat.

In a book of poems I find a postcard
of Marc's Tower of Blue Horses.
The beasts grow restless and immense
and transform this room into a stable almost
celestial. On the breast of one is fixed
the crescent moon like a brokn hoop.

As long as I abide my nature
there is no restraining them. They have no
notion of time for already their heads are turned
west and by eight they will vanish leaving
the scent of heaven threatening and stale.

On East Avenue
the ginkgoes shed their yellow leaves.
In the belfry of St. Andrew's Church
Quasimodo tolls the bells. It is noon.

Where do they come from,
the women, the children to play
catch-my-shadow with the vast
black shadow of the hunchback that trembles
under their feet
as they stamp and trace his shape?

   Augustine
   Theresa
   Joan
   St. Francis of Assisi
   pity the opaque shadow.

Allhallows Eve II

The children at the door look familiar
behind their masks.
Give them rice. You give them toffee
and they go away. In the living room,
friends warmed by the cheap wine sing
'Waly, Waly,' 'Waltzing Matilda' until
slowly, very slowly echos become fainter and fainter.
Rice, rice, rice, rice.

Over a year has passed since we met.
In the dark we talk of our childhoods.
You, of Mona who had Juno's breasts,
of sunrise over the Kaserstatt,
of Interlaken hidden by clouds,
of how when you were twenty-three.

You read a little about a summer in Freedom;
the mist on Loon Lake when the male
and female in me became enamoured of a bird
as it dove into the free springs below the surface.

There was a cemetery behind the farmhouse
we always passed on our way to the beach.
I found it by accident one afternoon
as I walked along the edge of the brook.

Black-eyed Susans broke out everywhere,
the yarrow and self-heal.
In places clumps of grass had split
stone markings of dead daughters and sons.
Snow and rain partially effaced
names and dates. But where the craftsman
etched deep into the stone, inscriptions
remained distinct and whole.

Lowell Towle
died
Aug. 3, 1891
AE 90 ys. 2 mos.
"All the days of my appointed time will I wait
till my change comes." Job 14-14

Mary
wife of L. T.
Died Mar. 4, 1892
AE 83 ys. 2 mos.

"I shall be satisfied, when
I awake with thy likeness." Ps. 17:15

An orange cat
stood poised upon a broken wall.
Swished its tail and glared at me before
leaping out of sight.

Letter From a School Friend

> Brussels, June 16th, 1965
> The Square Marie Louise

I have been in Belgium for two months.
It has been raining nearly every day.
Squeezed into an old armchair
I write. The monotony of the rain makes me sleepy
but I want to write to you.

I look out of the window
upon an artificial lake, trees lovely
in a big city.

This is an old Victorian house
with a room as high as in India,
a stucco ceiling, a fake chandelier
and a French bed deprived of use.

There are caves at the far shore of the lake
and the water cascades.
Old paths for lovers, old people,
are margined by chestnut trees.

Tirelessly I listen
to a fountain, to a girl with a lute
and am reminded of you looking
at Nefertiti or endlessly wishing
David would breathe.

Doves awaken me in the mornings.

I am told, in winter the seagulls
fly in from the sea.

Now there are ducks and carp
in the water and on Sundays
people, mushrooms, god knows,
lunar beings with blue umbrellas
go fishing or stroll along.

It must be wonderful to be so still
or are they stupid, such ordinary beings
to be sure without an 'intellectual type' among them?

I do not write for them but you.
Why do you agree to such a life?

Brussels is full. The rare medieval heart
of a city still in untidy colours.
The park has turned to summer
and the swans look green. Come see.

Every day I cross the market square
busy and open as an indian bazaar.
In the west the streets are named after professions.
One street sells nothing but antiquities.
There must be something for you
or have your tastes changed after America?

I am in love with a man
whose education is at odds with mine.
He is a beautiful person.

It has stopped raining.

On a clear night the trees' shadows have weight.

When I walk along the shores this summer
the lights are on at nine
but I know the grounds, not
whom I pass.

They taught us, the nuns, our parents that a beautiful
character is the highest goal: that the child will enter
the kingdom of heaven: the rich young man was turned down.
I choke. As a German I hate walls. In six months I will be
back in India to work among Tibetan refugees. Don't *you*
go back for noble causes.

After the rain
the air is sweet.
You ought to know,
I have almost forgotten.

I pray if there is something higher, I will be strong.

In Brussels the Indian girls are lovely
in their saris. When they walk
a city turns to stare.

Write
Love
Heidi.

                — for Heidrun
                    Grace
                  Patamaka
                  Nirmala

In Praise of the Beauty of Asian Women

Marisa Berenson, "the most beautiful girl in the world"!

But that is impossible!
(did I lapse from the colourless sky
with a defective passport?
A date of birth was given;
the names of town and country of origin.
a blank dotted line to indicate "world"
was just not there.
Perhaps a printing error.)

I thought that I went to school
with the most beautiful girl in the world:
Tin Tin Oo.

She spent summers in the Northern Provinces
and on holy days left her sandals
outside the Shwe Dagon.
Her shoulders brushed against
the gold leaf spire.

It was only when I accepted
that even my bones could not match hers,
was I able to pass the Cambridge
School Boards first class.
Not that she was vacuous or giggly.

After all she
decided to stay home in Yan Kon
on the east bank of the Hliang,
and bore pure-blooded children.

I see what you mean though,
in a sense.
A shape and face like Ms. Tiny's
is out of this world,
and the world ends at Haifa.
But until I am stripped of the memory
of such a face,
I have no cause to envy
any other in this world.

The Bondswoman: Three Poems

1

Everywhere I am, you are there,

but a mirror cracks
for leaner
desolate years.

Will a prophet arise when the dream is told?
What cattle chomped the summer
grass? Tell distinctly
of the milk that flowed
and nourished one for a year?

Hidden by Kedron
will ravens bring me bread,
crumbs, as I sing

of you and for nothing else?

2

What do
you want from me Lord?

When the old women rub their
stomachs in winter,
I am there.

When the third actor looks on the she
of success I am
there.

At the other's kiss of greeting
as the paralysed voyeur
I am there.

The wind pitches itself against the trees.
What at twenty-three understands despair?
Glass beads rumble against the sides
of the concave self, and lie still
at last, I am there.

Christ
in the dented funnel pour
silences.

3

Ill-bred I am caught
with my fingers in the butter,
my dress front wears the wine.
You have driven me back further than dreams.

There are leaves in my hair
and a song simpers and dies.
I think of this every day between
the trailers and the coffee-break.

'This is it. This is all.'
Others strike the eye of the fish
and receive the arcane herb year after year.
The grass leans to the wind, not my harmonica.

At night the trees dance on a borrowed bed.
I haven't wanted since June.
Lord, why do you *let* the poor?

I have been afraid before but today
I thought I had to live a thousand years.

Notes from Underground

They have locked me here since Friday night.
There is little privacy and no flowers.
Bring me some rain if you can.

The blue and white backs of women
disappear briefly for open toilets.
The halls are wide all right.
At one end there is an exhibit — art.
Kindergarten. "A large grackle with worm on grass."

Grass.
Has the grass changed much?

They feed us but the windows are wired.
The world I lately know is inside, crushed white.

Here is one who talks to herself and bums
cigarettes from me all day and a beauty
who will not talk. And here is one and here
is one. Here is one

saying to herself, who are these?
I already knew pain was not anonymous
and that no man is singled out for Eden.

My fingers ache to succeed on the piano.
Then, just then, these are persons
I have lived with all my life.
There is no word for them. Hands.

Why did you lead me here?
There isn't a thing on the walls.
At night when I don't think of you
I go to the Louvre or Rome

and steal Rembrandts and Davids
but stealing gives no pleasure
like the rare gratuitous gift.

And finally will you listen to this?

The elegant poplar can be downed
by one hurricane and a deified mountain
erupt; some hummingbirds may exchange
speed for higher flight; the sun
be dionysian.

When you do not come, or leave . . .
(by the way I prefer tamarisk to chrysanthemums.
Poor, poor Medea.)

Why does the scholar athenian sneer
at the spartan seeking knowledge
and the rich canaanite refuse
the tired egyptian room?

Because you show me nothing
I have to give

let me go,
a peasant with his only possessions,
his talisman — love, and the bright world
that sticks like a burr.

Monk's Girl in Two Perspectives

I'd rather tell this standing up
by the window. The wind
how it roars tonight. Out there
in the dark *he* waits impatiently
Don't repeat this to anyone. I'd die.

My apprentice eyes; these long thin arms
loose by my side, these bones — a man
couldn't have anything else to remember me by —
even this flat little voice.
He was much older. After it was done

I went to the window. The trees
were dark and great along the path. There was a
 moon.

I was naked then and stood just like this,
my arms wrapped about me, wrapped around
what was beautiful outside and in myself

in the cold and stranger's room. On a desk
was a typewriter, a copy of *Villon*.
The plaza lights swam near. I could almost
touch them and the scent of wet grass.
I felt as though a sad and thoughtful ghost

twenty centuries old had something to say.
 Afterwards
a girl ought never to cry I suppose.
But it was not for shame or fear. Perhaps I was
too thin or the shadow of a tree or the cry
a mad blind king once made when he hugged

his daughter in the snow. "Why" . . . ?
But he lay on the bed and never spoke a word.
He stared at the ceiling. He lay
basking in the moonlit glory of his body.
So I dressed myself and came away without a word.

New Year's Eve 1974

Beyond the scrubby junipers outside the window
there are terraces in the mind,
in the high peaks behind my eyes.
The mist climbs upwards to the high mountains,
taking with it the scent of fresh tea,
and the sun scorches Kanchenjunga,
and the sherpas smelling tea on the high slopes
grow drunk and blind and fall
into a crevasse on the far side,
the side of the holy city, Lhasa.

for Tenzing Norgay

Dusky Sally

As a young girl
in the evenings, no one came to me
but in dreams — from across the river,
out of a photograph or the pages
of a novel.

He leaned against the pillar
and engaged me in passionate conversations.
I was always ready
in a crisp new cotton sari everyday.
I was prepared —
to lose him in an accident or a war
or to a previous betrothal,
or we would grow apart, naturally.

Anyway, I had my pride left,
and that was something.

Asia

Somewhere a boat no bigger than my fist
overturns
and drowns everyone in it.

I do not attempt to save it.
Would you?
Being what I am? Knowing what I know?

Each night, when the red moon and the darkness
marry
I stand on this far shore and mark
with an X the places
where the bodies are washed up.

And I shoulder them one by one —
safe conduct
to the vaults in my memory,
where they may lie in state
beyond contempt and further violations.

I build fires on the crosses.
The smoke stretches across these rooms
to make a ring around me.

I shall never know any other
enchantment
but this part mourning.

So I watch my speech and dress,
and do not look long at a man.

Hour of Darkness, Hour of Light

We have talked late into the night.

The fire is an old man
and the lamp on the street
has burnt out.

I beg you before I leave,
if you have more wine,
serve it now;
if you have more to say,
say it quickly and be cunning,
even a little immoral —
shine a knife in my eyes and ask,
"Do you mean it? How does it feel?"

Or
trouble my high bed with kings and tell me
that saints with spinning wheels
shall visit me.

Speak to me of fellowship and the love of God.
Anything. Anything.
Sustain my hand.
Light this page.

Address before an Empty Assembly

Alif

It is enough . . . from the day I was born
in 1942 . . . it is enough.
My mother quickly voided her water
and when they weighed me I must have known,

(with the knowledge that has no mirror
and cannot see its own reflection;

with the knowledge that has no mouth
and therefore cannot sing or cry;

the knowledge without anvil or hammer.)

I was born
victim and terrorist
in equal parts.

Be

Shumbu,

because you are the only image of a God in this house,
and have endured the profanity of my Christian teachers,

tell me,
by whose scales does one measure suffering?

If my redemption can only come through suffering,
let me be damned.

If my redemption requires the death of one other
or six others,

I insist on being damned:
a cockroach, a grub.

But I will not forget to mourn. I will not forget.
But I will feel no more guilt.

Shumbu,

if my redemption cannot come from the work of my hands,
the ordinary breath of my small asian life,
by loving a man, by bearing a son,
by the presence
of friends at my table,
(and why not?)
of even my enemies . . .

Give me the courage to use your knife
and furrow into the deep earth of my own body
and see with the eye of a grub, a God dancing like a God
to the sound of my mere breath coming to a stop.

Te

After the first death . . .

I bring it all home.

Once there was a girl—

her soul popping out of her eyes.

She was so stupid that everytime
she gave herself to a man,
she'd say, "I trust you
because you are a poet or a liberal,
or if I'm very lucky, both."

Later she'd wipe off the spit
with a khadi washcloth — (pieces
of a grandmother's sari
from Independence days.)

and she'd chant, "Bapuji, I'm learning humility."

When she went into hiding,
I'd leave the back door open
and a bowl of rice and lentils
on the kitchen table at night.

She began talking funny:

"I sleep in the bosom of my father
who is older than Abraham."

Another time it was,

"Mohammed Darweesh,
I want to see your poems in the literary magazines of the US;
your picture on the front page of the APR."

She was sounding dangerous.
She couldn't find a job
and her poems returned with greater frequency.

Se

I showed her the PEN ad:

> *Members pledge themselves to oppose any form of suppression of freedom of expression in the country and community to which they belong.*

"That's the rub.
What country? What community?
Forsooth, what language?
Besides you've got to be
in a non-Western country.
I've thought of going to Russia,
of changing my religion,
of writing to Jerzy Kozinski.

> Dear Sir,
>
> You have not heard of me. One
> of the harassment tactics of the KGB
> is to make one unheard of. They
> don't even put my name on programs.
> *That's* harassment. But I am a very
> important closet poet. In fact,
> once I am in the West I shall be
> instantly recognized as the matriarch
> of the closet poets of the world.
>
> Sincerely,
> an endangered fellowpen,
> Olga Volga."

Poor girl, and over 5 years of shrinks too.
How can anyone believe her.

Jim

11 years now she's been dead.

No one gave her a bouquet of white lilacs.

I buried her in two pieces
as she'd asked:
her terrorist western head
is in the front yard
among the English daisies,
the gypsophila and delphinium.

Her victim body is rendered to dust
in the back under the hibiscus
rosa sinensis.

Twice a year
I turn over the earth
mixed with gypsum and manure.
The whole neighbour-
hood walks up and down in summer
to admire.

She sings at the top of her shrill
voice ragas for morning and evening.
No one listens anymore or understands
those eerie microtones, so she sings
for me, so I will not
forget my name and what I am
or from where I came, and go
inhuman
mad
not knowing.